DOLMABAHÇE PALACE

TBMM DEPARTMENT OF NATIONAL PALACES

DOLMABAHÇE PALACE

A PUBLICATION OF THE TBMM DEPARTMENT OF NATIONAL PALACES
İSTANBUL 1995

PUBLICATION NO. 14 OF THE TBMM DEPARTMENT OF NATIONAL PALACES

PUBLISHER ON BEHALF OF THE TGNA FOUNDATION TÜRKÂN İNCE (DIRECTOR OF DEPARTMENT OF NATIONAL PALACES)

MANAGING EDITOR AND COORDINATOR İHSAN YÜCEL (DEPUTY DEPARTMENT HEAD FOR CULTUR AND PRESENTATION)
DESIGN ERSU PEKİN
TEXT İHSAN YÜCEL, Dr. SEMA ÖNER
TRANSLATION MARY IŞIN
EDITORIAL TEAM AYDAN GÜRÜN, ESİN ÖNCÜ, YAŞAR YILMAZ, HAKAN GÜLSÜN, FERDA ULUGERGERLİ, DEMET AYGAR (CULTURAL-INFORMATION AND PUBLICATIONS OFFICE)
PHOTOGRAPHS FİKRET YILDIZ, SAMİH RİFAT, YILMAZ DİNÇ
TYPESETTING MİLLİ SARAYLAR BİLGİ İŞLEM MERKEZİ
COLOUR SEPERATION BAŞKENT GRAFİK
PRINTED BY TBMM BASIMEVİ
FIRST ADDITION 1989
SECOND ADDITION 1995

ISBN 975-7479-42-X

Contents

FOREWORD

The palaces which were not only the residences of the Ottoman sultans but centres of government for the Ottoman Empire, and the smaller köşks and kasırs which the sultans used for recreation became the property of the nation on 3 March 1924, shortly after the establishment of the Turkish Republic.

Today administered by the Department of National Palaces, which is directly attached to the Turkish Grand National Assembly, these imperial buildings are known collectively as the National Palaces and open to the public as museum-palaces. They are each a highly significant focal point of history, throwing light on the social structure, government, art and culture of Ottoman society.

Obtaining detailed and reliable knowledge of these buildings, which were not only residences of the Ottoman sultans but centres of government until the early years of this century, depends on extensive research. This is the second addition of Dolmabahçe Palace which was printed in 1989 for the first time includes its role in Ottoman administrative structure, social life, culture and art. Reference to this information in future publications will undoubtedly help to bring to light further details about İstanbul's other imperial buildings.

I hope that readers will enjoy this book, and that further planned National Palaces publications will play a role in the understanding and conservation of our national heritage. I also take this opportunity to thank all those who have contributed to its publication.

TÜRKÂN İNCE
Director
Department of National Palaces

THE THIRD OTTOMAN IMPERIAL GRAND PALACE IN İSTANBUL

During the six hundred years of Ottoman rule, the seat of the empire changed several times, from Bursa to Edirne and later to İstanbul. The site of the imperial 'palace', center of Ottoman government, changed also over the centuries in İstanbul itself. The earliest palace to post-date the Ottoman conquest of İstanbul was the *Saray-ı Atik-i Âmire* (the Old Palace - 1453/1478). After which the Ottoman imperial seat of government removed, at some point, to Topkapı Palace, known as the *Saray-ı Cedid-i Âmire* (Built between 1478 and 1856). In subsequent eras, the sultans inhabited *Topkapı, the Çırağan Palace, the shore palace at Beşiktaş and Beylerbeyi Palace* at various intervals, until the completion of Dolmabahçe Palace in 1856, when this became the official Ottoman seat.

In 1877 the sultan moved once again, this time to Yıldız Palace, where the Ottoman court remained until 1909. From that date until the dissiolution of the sultanate in 1922, Dolmabahçe regained its status as official imperial residence.

The Palace of Dolmabahçe, completed in 1856, is the third largest Ottoman Palace in İstanbul. It embodies, in its very form the social and cultural structure of the period, of which it is stylistically typical.

Dolmabahçe was a prestigious addition to the urban silhouette of İstanbul built on a prominent site at the entrance to the Bosphorus. It stands at a focal point in the fast growing 19th century city, and was built at a time of increasing enthusiasm for all things occidental.

Here for the first time was a building resulting from the detailed plannig rather than the organic principle of growth in response to need, as had been the case in Topkapı Palace.

Certain structural additions, unusual for Ottoman royal buildings were made to Dolmabahçe in keeping with the trends of the time, such as the palace theatre-the Saray-ı Hümâyûn Tiyatrosu.

The main building of the palace is set parallel to the Bosphorus and surrounded by high walls. It is of a self-sufficient

Sultan Abdülmecid, who built Dolmabahçe Palace. From Fihrist-i Şâhân in Süleymaniye Library.

9

complex including annexes serving all the social and administrative needs of the palace.

The main building is, in fact, to sections, the administrative and private quarters; the former for men only-Mabeyn-i Hümâyûn, which-and the women's quarters-the Harem-i Hümâyûn, which are joined under one roof with access from one section to the other via the Grand Ceremonial Hall- the Muayede Salon. The Heirs Elected Apartments - Veliahd Daire - is an extansion of the main building which adjoines the sprawling palace further along the shore, although in fact it was cut off from the main building by a high wall seperating this wing of the palace from the Harem. It is today the Mu-

seum of Art and Sculpture of Mimar Sinan University. In its basic layout, the palace attempted to reconcile some increasingly popular western elements with Ottoman architectural tradition and with oriental social tradition. The decoration both on the exterior and within reflects an elaborate, heavily eclectic westernised aesthetic.

The immediate environment of the palace is known to have been one of the ancient settlement. It is thought that the ancient mythical vessel the *Argos* visited these shores, and throughout the classical era the area was known as *Iasonion*, after *Jason* the captain of Argos.

During the Byzantine period, a palace, hippodrome and oth-

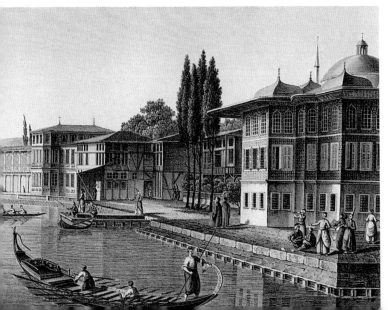

facing page above *Dolmabahçe Valley in 1810. Drawing by Préault in Promenades Pittoresques dans Constantinople by Charles Pertusier.* above *Dolmabahçe as seen from the cemetery in Pera in the 1830s. Drawing by Bartlett in Julia Pardoe's Beauties of the Bosphorus.* left *Beşiktaş Waterfront Palace which previously occupied the site of Dolmabahçe Palace. The building on the far right is Çinili Köşk. Engraving by Melling in Voyage Pittoresque de Constantinople et des Rives du Bosphore, Paris 1819, Plate 28, TSM Library.*

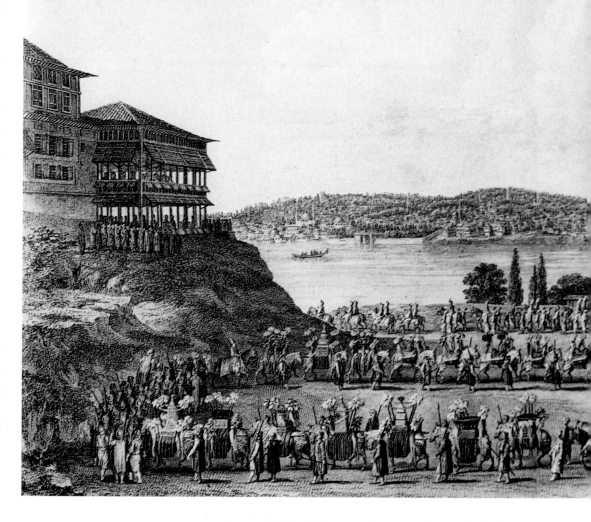

er large public buildings were known to have existed along the shore between Kabataş and Beşiktaş.

Ottoman sources reveal that this remained a popular site after the conquest of İstanbul, when mosques, fountains and pavilions were built along the shore at various times.

The actual site of the Palace of Dolmabahçe was formerly a harbour, the traditional last moorage of the imperial fleet before the start of a campaign, up to the 17th century.

Previous imperial palace buildings occupied the shore at "Beşiktaş" and around the bay of *Dolmabahçe*, until in the 17th century, the bay, which had become silted up was filled in completely. The newly acquired shore was given the name Dolmabahçe - "infill gardens". The task of filling this huge bay was begun in 1614 during the reign of Ahmet I (1613-1617) by Halil Paşa, Admiral of the Fleet, by order of Grand Vizier Na-

suh Paşa. Infill work was finally completed in the reign of Osman II.

In his famous book of travels, the 17th century chronicler, Evliya Çelebi mentions the area as small cypress grove bordering on a bay which when it became silted up was filled in by order of Osman II. The sultan ordered the entire Ottoman fleet, together with 20.000 kayıks and barges from the port of İstanbul to fill the bay, creating an area of 400 arşıns (approximately 400 yards) of land.

The infill area linked up imperial groves in Beşiktaş and Kabataş, the Hasbahçe and *Karaabalı* groves. These were gradually enhanced by pavilions and royal lodges and the whole shoreline remained among the most favoured imperial estates for centuries. Some royal pavilions and lodges are known to have existed around the by before it became infilled, one of the

above **The Sürre Alayı carrying gifts to Mecca on sacred camels in the 1790s. The building on the left is Bayıldım Köşkü. From D'Ohsson's account of the Ottoman Empire.**
following pages **Dolmabahçe Palace in 1875. The palace is newly built and the clock tower has not yet been constructed. Oil painting by Luigi Querena. Private collection.**

13

above *Dolmabahçe Palace from Gümüşsuyu hill. Oil painting by an anonymous artist. Dolmabahçe Palace collection.*

earliest among them being the Kaptan Paşa Yalısı, later renamed the *Cağalıoğlu Yalısı*. This was used by Beyazıt II (1481-1512). Sources for the reign of Süleyman I refer to the area as a favorite imperial resort, the gardens and groves of which were famous (notably the Karaabalı Mehmet Baba groves). According to Evliya Çelebi, during the reign of Selim II (1566-1574) the only structure there was a royal lodge and pool built by that sultan. Ahmet I (1603-1617) is known to have constructed a pavilion although it is uncertain how long that building remained intact.

A considerable amount of construction took place during the reign of Mehmet IV (1648-1687), with the resulting complex being known as the Beşiktaş Shore Palace. One building of par-

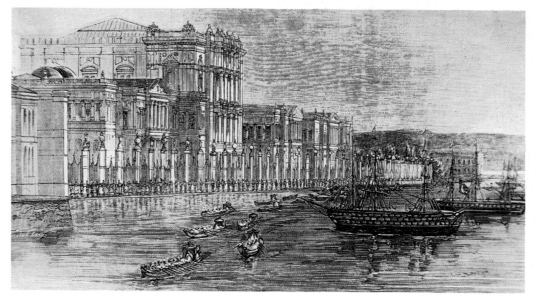

ticular renown dating from this period (now no longer extant) was the Çinili Pavilion-Çinili Köşk (dated 1678-1680).

The existing palace buildings were extended and restored during the reign of Ahmet III (1703-1730). The pavilions and garden enclosure of Dolmabahçe, which were reputedly in ruins in 1719, were restored and incorporated into the Beşiktaş Palace complex at that time, when the imperial estates were enclosed by high walls. The entire complex and its grounds were renamed the Imperial Palace of Beşiktaş - *Beşiktaş Saray-ı Hümâyûnu*. Subsequently, during the reign of Mahmut I, a series of pavilions known as the *Bayıldım Köşks* were built on the slopes above the Dolmabahçe estates (dating to 1748).

A mausoleum from the same period which now stands

above *Postcard depicting Dolmabahçe Palace as seen from the hillside Fındıklı at the turn of the 20th century.*
below *Palace women going by caique from Dolmabahçe Palace to Topkapı Palace during the reign of Sultan Abdülaziz. L'Illustration, 10 June 1876.*
following pages *Dolmabahçe Palace in the late 19th century. The building in the foreground is the Hamlahane, which no longer stands today. By Jean Brindesi, from Souvenirs de Constantinople.*

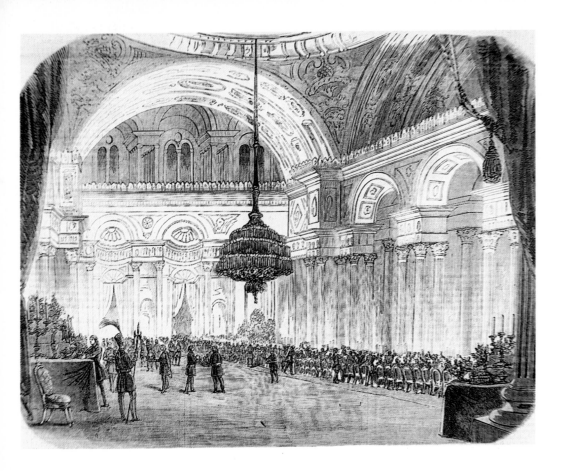

Banquet held in honour of Marshal Pélissier in the Ceremonial Hall of Dolmabahçe Palace shortly after it was completed. L'Illustration, 7 April 1877.

within the grounds of Dolmabahçe Palace, containing the sarcophagi of the wives and daughters of Mahmut I, indicates that the shore palace was inhabited at this time.

The Beşiktaş Palace was inhabited over the second of the 18th century, when various additions were made to the structure and continious restoration took place during the reigns of Osman III (1754-1757), Abdülhamid I (1774- 1789) and finally Selim III (1789- 1807).

By the turn of the century, royal buildings stretched along the shore from Beşiktaş to Defterdar Burnu, beginning with the Saray-ı Hümâyûn at Beşiktaş and extending to the Hatice Sultan Palace at Defterdar Burnu. The European shores of the Bosphorus had become the most sought after of sites for the awellings of the Sultan and his retinue.

Accounts of restorations made during the reign of Selim III to the Beşiktaş Palace refer to various pavilions and lodges by name, so that we know there existed at that time a Kasr-ı Cedid, the Valide Sultan Dairesi, the Kasr-ı Hümâyûn-ı Tâcidarî and the Sahilhane -i Hümâyûn among others. Mahmut II (1808-1839) ordered the thorough restoration of the palace on

his accession, to be carried out by the Imperial Architect -Baş
Mimar Hafız Mehmed Emin Efendi. The restoration was begun
in 1809. On its completion, Mahmut II began to reside in the
new palace as well as Topkapı.

Opening ceremony for the Ottoman parliament held in the Ceremonial Hall at Dolmabahçe Palace on 19 March 1877. L'Illustration.

During the reign of his son Abdülmecid (1839-1861), some
of the pavilions belonging to the Beşiktaş Palace were demol-
ished to make way for a new palace complex.

The imperial command to begin the new palace building
was issued by Abdülmecid once a sizeable site had been
cleared, in 1842-1843.

The main building was the first part of the palace to be completed, as the inscription medallion bearing the sultan's seal
and the date 1847 (H. 1263) within the pendentive over the
main portal informs us. A carved seal with the same date is to
be found on the façade of the same building, which houses the
public section of the palace-the Mabeyn-i Hümâyûn.

Similar seals and dates scattered throughout the complex
give clear indication of the chronology of the palace's construction, successive dates fix the Imperial Gate-Saltanat Kapı as being finished earliest (in 1854/H. 1270) followed by the Dowe-

ger Sultan Gate-Valide Kapısı in 1855 (H.1271) and the Treasury Gate Hazine Kapı between 1855-1856 (H.1272). These dates show that the walls and gates of the palace were completed later than the main structure. Certainly it appears that the palace itself was completed gradually, stage by stage, and the construction as a whole seems to have lasted from 1842-1856.

The French writer Théophile Gautier relates how he was shown around the palace by one of the architects of the building, Garabet Balyan in 1853, when the interior was still being decorated. He also mentions that he was first shown a number of old buildings before they were pulled down.

The palace building and decoration were completed by 1856, according to the daily press Ceride-i Havadis of 11 June 1856 (7 Şevval 1272). An article printed in the press tells us that Abdülmecid took up residence in the palace on 7 June, (3 Şevval) and summoned his ministers on the following they do discuss the affairs of state, financial problems in particular. Discussing the latter, he is reported as saying: *"The conviction that an increase in income should mean an increase in outlay at a time when the Ottoman dominions are yielding no revenue is disastrous, it is the road to ruin. The palace is sumptuous, it could have been less elaborate."* When faced with the protestations of a member of court, who said *"But my lord this is but little for you"*, the Sultan replied: *"No, no, I also feel that this was extravagant."*

Abdülmecid remained in the palace a very short time before his death. He was succeeded by Abdülaziz (1866-1876) who also resided in Dolmabahçe until his deposition and the succession of Murat V (1876). The sultanate of the latter was extremely short, ending in his deposition three months later and the succession of Abdülhamid II (1876-1909). The latter sultan remained in Dolmabahçe only one month before moving to Yıldız Palace for greater security. He remained there until his deposition. In 1909, Mehmet V came to the throne, and moved back into Dolmabahçe after having it renovated by one of the leading architects of the day, Vedat Tek. On the date of Mehmet V in 1918, his successor Mehmet VI (Vahdettin) (1918-1922) remained in Dolmabahçe for a certain time before moving to Yıldız Palace. It was from the jetty of Dolmabahçe that he was to leave Türkiye in 1922.

Subsequently, Abdülmecid Efendi, last of the Ottomans was installed in Dolmabahçe Palace as caliph on 18 November 1922, but with the abolation of the caliphate he was removed from the palace and left the country with his family.

Finally, a law passed on 3 March, 1924 on the directive of Atatürk (Law no. 431) declared the estates and possessions of the imperial family, including Dolmabahçe Palace and all the imperial pavilions, mansions and lodges to be part of the National Heritage.

THE BUILDING

Théophile Gautier, visiting the site before the completion of the palace in 1853 recorded his opinions on it his work "İstanbul":

"It is difficult to identify a particular architectural style. The palace is neither Greek, nor Roman, Gothic, Renaissance nor Arabesgue, nor is it Turkish. The obsessively-worked detail of intricate decoration and ornamentation recall that of a Spanish monument in the so-called Lateresco style."

left *The seaward façade of the palace from the minaret of Dolmabahçe Mosque.*
below *Garabet Balyan, architect of Dolmabahçe Palace.*

The white façade of the palace stretching along the Bosphorus shore. Bezm-i Âlem Valide Sultan (Dolmabahçe) Mosque and the clock tower can be seen in the background.

The style of the palace has, in fact, been variously interpreted by different sources of the period. It was the product of eclecticizm. The plan bears both Occidental and Turkish features, while the ornamentation both inside and out reveals Baroque, Roccoco and Empire features which have been skillfully amalgamated in one building by the Ottoman architects.

Many notable artists and architects in both the Ottoman and European traditions worked on the structure and decoration of the palace.

The chief architect was Garabet Balyan, who was assisted by Nikogos Balyan, the latter being responsible for the construction of the Ceremonial Hall-Muayede Salon, and two gates, the

above *View of the palace from Beşiktaş.*
below *View of the palace from Dolmabahçe.*

the Imperial Gate-Saltanat Kapı, and the Treasury Gate-Hazine-i Hassa Kapı.

The main building of the palace is divided into three sections, the administrative-Mabeyn-i Hümâyûn, the Ceremonial Hall-Muayede-i Hümâyûn, and the private apartments of the sultan and his family the Harem-i Hümâyûn. The centrally placed grand hall, which rose through the two main stories of

the palace, was flanked on either side by two wings set parallel to the shoreline, the first being the administrative, the second the private wing. The Harem occupies a considerable amount of the site,finally extending inland at right-angles to the shore.

The palace is actually three storeys throughout if we include the lower service floor and the gallery flanking the upper storey of the Muayede Salon.

The general plan is, in fact, identical to that of the typical Turkish dwelling, with a central public area-the sofa- flanked by rooms leading off to each side. It has simply been carried out on an extremely grand scale.

However, each section of the palace has been independently designed around the same principle, the concept of individual areas in western fashion being integrated with the features of a typical Turkish architectural plan.

The three main functional areas of the palace are collected under one roof in a most unusual arrangement for Turkish architecture. The palace contains a total of 285 rooms, 43 halls, 6 terraces and 6 hamams (Turkish baths) over a total area of 14.595 m^2. The façades are pierced by 1427 windows and there are 25 doors to the palace, each with a different function, giving access from the shore and gardens. The building is based on a foundation of timber posts embedded into the infill, overlaid with a timber grid infilled with a layer of rough cement-Horasan Harcı- 1m-1.20m deep. There are three rows of tim-

facing page above *Aerial view of the palace.*
below *The seaward façade.*

Façade of the Mabeyn.

bers throughout the grid over which the buildings were constructed. The walls of the palace are stone with brick infill-frame and faced with ashlar. They support a roof of timber surfaced with lead. Over the Muayede Salon, the timber sloping roof acts as a most unusual outer membrain for the dome covering the hall, while the crystal staircase in the Mabeyn-i Hümâyûn is vaulted over with a glass roof. The interior structure-walls, ceilings etc. are wood.

Various kinds of coarse sandstone were used on the façades along-side stone from Marseille and Trieste. Marble too, is employed, generally local marble from the Marmara. In the sultan's bath Egyptian alabaster covers the walls and floors. The structural timbers are mainly pine and oak, together with some African and Indian woods.

Purplish glass was used for the windows to protect the decoration and furnishings of the palace. This is said to prevent ultraviolet rays from passing through the glass.

THE DECORATION

The striking decorations one may see throughout the palace both on the exterior and the interior are a blend of western styles of various periods. On the façades we see cartouches, rosettes, medallions, oyster shells, wreaths and garlands, vases and "C" and "S" shaped scrolls in Baroque, Rococo and Empire styles merged into one composition, giving the whole façade an eclectic appearance.

Ottoman art was no stranger to these styles, and individual buildings exist as proof of their adoption as separate styles over the years in İstanbul, but Dolmabahçe is the first building

Window grilles on the basement floor.

above *Detail of the exterior decoration.*
below *Detail of the decoration on the*
steps leading up to the Ceremonial Hall.
facing page *One of the pairs of windows*
on the seaward façade.

in which they were amalgamated to such effect.

A similar eclecticism can be seen on the interior of the palace. Motifs from the façade recur on the interior walls and ceilings, but interspersed with cartouches containing trompe d'oeil paintings, still lives, animal figures and landscapes. These are mainly painted on plaster and plaster of Paris, sometimes on wood, canvas, lead and glass. Some of the ceilings are cassetted, each cassette bearing different decorations. Gold leaf and gilt is used throughout the interior, particularly on the casetted ceilings. Plaster mouldings are also an important feature of the interior. Trompe d'oeil is used on a grandscale on some walls and ceilings to considerable effect, creating false architectural spaces in several areas of the palace.

The traditional motifs of Ottoman polychrome tracery were augmented from the

mid-18th century onwards by Baroque and Rococo devices, which were increasingly used along side landscape painting both in Dolmabahçe and in a number of buildings contemporary to it in the Ottoman capital.

ORNAMENTS AND FURNISHING

We know that the designer of the Paris Opera, Séchan was in-
volved in the ornamentation and furnishing of Dolmabahçe. In
fact, there is evidence that he was responsible for the decoration of a group of rooms including the sultan's suite. Docu-
ments concerning payment to the artist indicate the terms un-

der which he was paid and also tell us that he received an imperial award, a fourth degree Mecidiye order from
Abdülmecid. We also learn from Théophile Gautier that Séchan's furniture workshop in Turgot was making furniture in
the Louise XIV style on order for one hall in the palace.

Much of the palace is covered with parquet flooring, some
of which is very intricate. The more basic parquet is of dark
and light oak arranged in cruciform interlace, creating square

facing page *The bed made by Séchan for
Sultan Abdülmecid.*
above *Detail of the parquet floor in
one of the rooms.*

floor panels, while the more elaborate flooring employs walnut, balsam, lime wood and other woods in intricate geometrical interlace patterns with foliate motifs. The doors, of mahogany and walnut are also decorated with marquetry. Furniture throughout the palace is largely of various European styles.

Some furniture was made by order for the palace while it was under construction, while other pieces were gifts from other European countries, and Far Eastern countries such as China, India and Egypt. Hence one may see artefacts and furniture of several different styles and origins in one room, while Turkish traditional seating-floor cushions-may also be seen.

Turkish fabrics were used throughout for the furnishings, mainly pure silks woven on the imperial looms at Hereke.

Most of the rugs are also from Hereke, although there are also some from the Feshane looms, and Kayseri and Uşak. Some valuable Iranian rugs are among those in the palace collection.

facing page and above *Examples of the palace furniture.*

There is a total of 142 rugs and 115 prayer rugs, covering a total surface of 4500 m².

One of the most noticeable features of the palace is the widespread use of crystal, particularly Baccarat and Bohemian crys-

tal chandeliers, although some of Beykoz crystal are also to be seen. There are 36 crystal chandeliers and 581 crystal and silver candelabra as well as a number of crystal-faced mantelpieces, candelabra of crystal and crystal balustrades. All the mirrors are crystal too.

Among the most interesting artefacts in the palace are the vases of which there are a total of 280. 46 of these are Yıldız Porcelain Factory ware. Others include 59 Chinese ware, 26 Japanese ware and 29 Sèvres ware. The others are from various Eurepean countries. Much of this ware was acquired as gifts.

The palace collection of clocks is also of considerable value. There are 159 clocks of various kinds, both local and European in origin.

facing page *A Thonet newspaper stand. This must have been purchased at a later date.*
above *One of the doors of the Süfera Salon.*
following page left *One of the vases in the Süfera Salon.*
following page right *Vase in the Medhal Salon.*

above *Picture of Dolmabahçe Palace in a ceiling frieze in the Harem.* facing page *Sèvres vase bearing the monogram of Abdülmecid.*

The Dolmabahçe collection of paintings is particularly noteworthy. Oils, water colours and works in other techniques include the work of both Turkish and European artists. The subjects are varied. Much of this collection was acquired during the reign of Abdülaziz, under the direction of sultan's art advisor the artist Şeker Ahmet Paşa, among whose acquisitions are the works of Daubigny, Schreyer, Fromentin and Gérome. Prominent in the collection are 30 oil paintings by Aivazovsky, who was at the Ottoman court before and during the reign of Abdülaziz, and 19 works in various techniques by Zonaro who was court artist to Abdülhamid II. Turkish artists are also well represented, among them are a number of military artists, namely Yüzbaşı Ali Rıza, Kolağası Hasan Behçet, and Şeker Ahmet Paşa and others, notably Halife Abdülmecid, Osman Hamdi Bey, and Hikmet Onat, all of whome were considered forerunners of Turkish painting.

LIGHTING AND HEATING

When the palace was first built, it was illuminated by gaslight, which was piped, imported especially for the palace from Great Britain, from a specially constructed gas works which stood on the site of the present Dolmabahçe Stadium (İnönü Stadium). Up to 1873-the gas works was run by the Imperial Treasury-Hazine-i Hassa İdaresi, after which it was taken over by a French gas company and subsequently by the İstanbul municipality. During the reign of Abdülmecid, steps were taken to introduce public gas lighting throughout the city, under the sultan's direction.

Later, the chandeliers and light fitments in the palace were converted to electiricity. This system remains in the palace today.

Various different methods of heating were used throughout

facing page *Reception room thought to have belonged to the Valide Sultan in the Harem.*
left *The fireplace in the antechamber of the Süfera Salon. The central heating system was installed during the reign of Mehmed Reşad.*

Detail of the fireplace in the antechamber of the Süfera Salon.

the palace over the years. Many halls and rooms have fireplaces, which was the main source of heating, while some rooms were heated by porcelain stoves and braziers.

The grand hall of the palace was, however, heated by an un-
derground system by which hot air was filtered from the cellar
below the hall through grills at the base of pillars in the hall,

*Detail of the fireplace in the Red
Room.*

providing a mean temperature of $18\text{-}20^0$. Later, during the reign of Mehmed V (Reşad) central heating was installed throughout the palace.

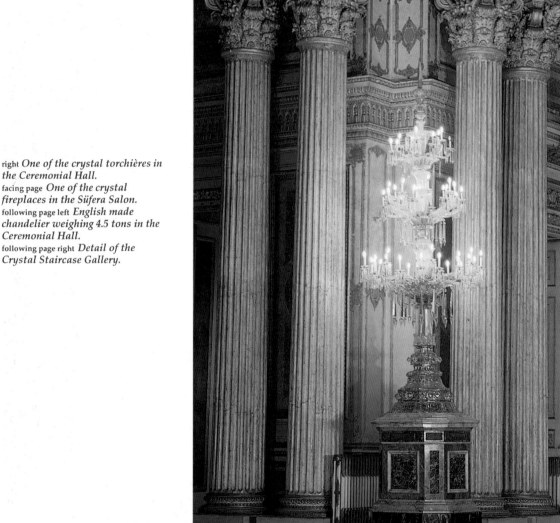

right *One of the crystal torchières in the Ceremonial Hall.*
facing page *One of the crystal fireplaces in the Süfera Salon.*
following page left *English made chandelier weighing 4.5 tons in the Ceremonial Hall.*
following page right *Detail of the Crystal Staircase Gallery.*

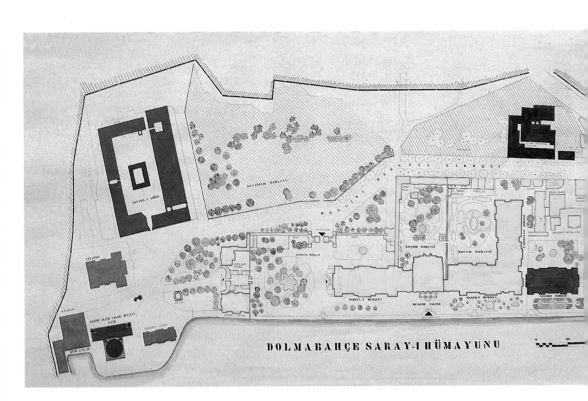

DOLMABAHÇE SARAY-I HÜMAYUNU

THE PLAN

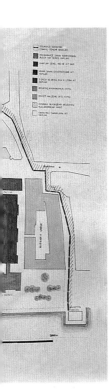

Dolmabahçe Palace is actually a vast complex of auxiliary buildings surrounding the main structure. Some remain within the walls of the palace, other related bulidings are to be found beyond the walls.

The following apartments and suites are to be found within the main building and throughout its annexes.

1 Chambers of the Imperial Treasury, 2 Furnishing Chambers, 3 Main Building: Mabeyn-i Hümâyûn, Muayede Salonu, Harem-i Hümâyûn, 4 Glazed Pavilion, 5 The Aviary, 6 Inner Treasury, 7 Kitchen, 8 Cellar, 9 Carpenters' workshop, 10 Apartments of the Heirs Elect, 11 Hareket Köşks, 12 Gedikli Cariyes' Apartments,

13 Chief Eunuchs' Apartments, 14 Hereke Weawing workshop, 15 Gentlemen in waiting's Apartments, 16 Agavat Apartments, 17 Servants' Apartments, 18 Guards Apartments, 19 The Imperial kitchen,

The following annexes were situated outside of the main walls.

20 Hamlahane, 21 Bezm-i Âlem Valide Sultan Mosque, 22 Saray-ı Hümâyûn Theatre, 23 Imperial mews and stables, 24 Clock tower, 25 Auxiliary service bulidings: a. Aviary, b. Furnishing and supplies stores (2), c. Şehzade Kemaleddin Efendi's kitchen, d. Guards' barracks, e. Old Laundry, f. Disused press, g. Ruined barracks, h. Stables, ı. Mill, j. Disused stable, k. Bakery dormitory, l. Disused kitchen (2), m. Yusuf İzzeddin Efendi Kitchen, n. Imperial confectioners, o. Imperial pharmacists, 26 Leased property-Akaretler.

facing page above *Aerial view of Dolmabahçe Palace.*
left *Plan of the Dolmabahçe Palace complex.*

THE PALACE WALLS AND GATES

The palace is enclosed by high stone walls on the land side and delicate wrought iron walls on the shore façade. The castle enclosure type battlemented walls traditional to Turkish palaces are thus employed here with some flexibility. It is a 19th century solution to the problem of seclusion.

The palace has a number of gates whose size and the elaborateness of whose ornamentation varies according to their function and importance.

THE LAND GATES
TREASURY GATE-HAZİNE KAPI

One of the most important means of access to the palace this gate is situated between the Imperial Treasury chambers-Hazine-i Hassa Dairesi and the Mefruşat Daire (Furnishing Chamber). It bears the function of linking the two abovementioned sections of the palace together physically in one

structure.

The portal itself fronts a round arched, barrel-vaulted porti-co. The double panelled gate is of ornate moulded iron, origi-nally said to have been gilded. Flanking the portal on either side are paired fluted columns with composite capitals. These are flanked in turn by blind arches with columns on either side; surmounted by a crenellated finial. From these curve out large

facing page The Treasury Gate at Dolmabahçe Palace.
above Inscription with the monogram of Abdülmecid dated AH 1272 over the Treasury Gate.
below The Treasury Gate depicted on an old postcard, showing that the gate used to be gilded.

Constantinople - Portes du Palais Im...

wings surmounted by towers. Each of these wings is pierced by a door which gives access to the Hazine-i Hassa and The Mefruşat Daire courtyards, while the towers also contain a door giving access to the court. The portal extends into three storeys within the tower, thus creating on independent functional space. The main decorations of the gate tend to be in the form of oyster shells, catouches garlands and pearl moulding, and vase-shaped finials.

An oval medallion on the crenellated section above the gate bears the tughra-monogram of Abdülmecid with an inscription dated 1855-1856 (H. 1272) in a rectangular panel below. The

above *Detail of the Treasury Gate.*
facing page above *The Imperial Gate as depicted on an old postcard.*
facing page below *The Imperial Gate from the sultan's private garden.*

inscription bears the signature of Şair Ziver, and contains his couplets.

The upper storey of the Hazine-i Hassa Chamber is linked to the upper storey corridor of the Treasury Gate via a vaulted corridor which also give access to the Mefruşat Dairesi. From the latter another corridor gives access to galleries within the palace enclosure walls, which are in fact double walls with a corridor within, running the length of the walls. The inner wall overlooking the palace grounds are pierced by windows up to the Imperial Gate, at which point the corridor terminates.

THE IMPERIAL GATE-SALTANAT KAPI

One of the most imposing of the palace gates, it leads from what was the Bayıldım Groves into the imperial grounds Hasbahçe. The gate itself is an elaborate cast-iron filigree double gate set into a round arched vaulted portal. It is   flanked

Constantinople - Entrée du Palais Impérial

on either side by fluted columns with composite capitals. Above are panels containing medallions surmounted by finialled double columns.

The portal is flanked by two curved concave wings, both on the outer and inner façade, which terminate in two towers. Above the gate is the tughra of Sultan Abdülmecid. The deco-

rative motifs are similar in style to those of the Hazine Kapı (Treasury Gate). The walls beyond this gate conceal a corridor leading to the Bendegân Kapı (Slaves Gate) and from there via the Camlı Köşk-Glazed Pavilion-a secret passageway leads to the main palace ending near the Muayede Salon (the Grand Ceremonial Hall).

The Hasbahçe (the sultan's private garden) seen from the Imperial Gate.

THE SLAVES GATE-BENDEGÂN KAPISI

This entrance has a glazed wooden door which leads into a broad passageway set at right angles to the main palace.

The passageway gives access both to the Camlı Köşk and to the palace proper. Towards the köşk, a second entrance to this two-storeyed structure gives access to the Aviary Gate-Kuşluk Kapısı. The passage wall separates the aviary from the imperial grounds and encloses and conceals it from public view.

THE AVIARY GATE-KUŞLUK KAPISI

This gate opens into the imperial aviary and joins the passageway leading to the Camlı Köşk. It is flanked by a horse block. The palace wall surrounding the aviary runs parallel to the palace and the shoreline until it meets the Harem wall. The aviary enclosure wall separates it from the Harem, and the outer wall becomes higher at this point, continuing the length of the Harem gardens, only to lose some height at the point where a carpentry workshop abuts onto it inside the grounds. Only one gate gives access to the Harem at this point the Dowager Sultan Gate (Valide Kapısı).

THE DOWEGER SULTAN GATE - VALİDE KAPISI

This arched portal is decorated with rectangular marble panels. It has a double door and is finely embellished both
on and above the door panels. The tughra of Sultan Abdülmecid may be seen in a medallion over the keystone, along with
the date-1855 (H. 1271). The palace wall continues past the Valide Kapı to the Harem Kapı.

THE HAREM GATE - HAREM KAPISI

This is a dressed stone entrance with wooden doors. Beyond this gate are several others leading to the *Veliahd
Dairesi*-apartments of the heirs elect, the *Baltacılar Dairesi*-Gu-
ardroom and the imperial kitchens-*Matbah-ı Âmire*. Here the
wall turns at right angles to the shore, and access to the rema-
inder of the palace grounds is via the *Musahiban Kapısı*-the ser-
vant's gate.

IMPERIAL SHORE GATES

There are five shore gates on the sea façade of the palace.
These are oval, cast iron filigree gates leading down to
the waterfront via flights of steps. The middle gate is the İmpe-
rial Shore Gate-*Saltanat Deniz Kapı*- and is larger than the ot-

facing page *The waterfront gate in the
Mabeyn garden.*
below *The same waterfront gate as
seen from the sea, with the Imperial
Gate in the background.*

hers. It is set directly in front of the Muayede Salon. The other gates are identical coronated cast-iron filigree structures flanked by fluted columns with composite capitals and decorated with foliate motifs framed by medallions and cartouches. A cast iron railing links the various gates and is punctuated by decorative columns. The gate closest to the main entrance to the Mabeyn-public quarters- is the Visieral Jetty Gate-*Vezir İskelesi Kapısı*.

below *The waterfront gate in front of the Ceremonial Hall.*
facing page *View of the same gate from the seaward façade.*

THE GARDENS

During the process of filling in the bay between the Beşiktaş Hasbahçe and the Karaabalı Garden at Kabataş, these two spacious gardens were linked up with the Bayıldım Gardens up the slope from the site of the palace. This created an extremely extensive estate, which now has the palace in the center of it while the gardens remaining within the present palace walls are European in their design, the Bayıldım Gardens to the west of the palace retained their Turkish character.

The palace gardens are in five main different areas.

facing page *The Mabeyn Hasbahçe Garden.*
below *The Hasbahçe in an old postcard.*

IMPERIAL GARDEN-HASBAHÇE

K nown as the public-Mabeyn or Selamlık gardens, they stretch from the Treasury Gate to the entrance to the palace. They are rectangular in layout-almost square, and are set at right angles to the palace entrance. The plan is dominated by a central pool surrounded by two concentric circles. The flanking spaces are bedded with plants and trees. The landscaping bears much European influence.

facing page *The ornamental pool in the Hasbahçe.*
above left *Detail of the same pool.*
above right *One corner of the Hasbahçe.*
below *The fountain in the form of a swan was brought here from Yıldız Palace gardens.*

facing page *The Hasbahçe pool.*
above *One of the statues in the Hasbahçe.*

left *One of the castiron lanterns in the palace gardens.*
facing page *The pool behind the Mabeyn.*

AVIARY GARDEN-KUŞLUK

This is to the land side of the Muayede Salon, and is so named as it contains an aviary and observation pavilion. It is more enclosed than the Hasbahçe. European influence is to be felt in the geometrical beds and the use of a pool.

HAREM GARDEN

This is contained within the enclosure formed by the "L" - shaped harem wing of the palace to the land side. Its main features bear some resemblance to those of the other gar-

dens, with an oval pool and geometrical beds.

The fourth and final section of the grounds are the gardens set between the Veliahd Daire and their annexes, and the Harem gardens. There is a fifth section which is contained by the garden walls, this being the servants' apartments-Bendegân and Musahiban Daire, and certain service buildings.

The Mabeyn garden extends along the shore façade of the palace, so that the palace appears from the sea to have a single continuous garden behind filigree iron railings.

This delicatel decorated railing is punctuated by regular posts bearing foliate finials.

Again here the landscaping emphasis is on geometry. The imperial quay gate is flanked on either side by a pond and there is a pool in the Veliahd Dairesi Gardens.

Throughout the gardens are features reminiscent of Europe-

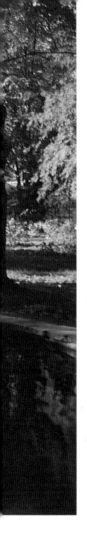

an gardens such as geometric beds, the use of garden statuary and jardiniers and garden lanterns but above all the overall garden design. One of the main reasons for this was that many of the gardeners and landscapists working on the Ottoman estates were from western Europe. During the reign of Abdülmecid, for example, the head gardener was a German named Sester, and his assistants were also German-Fritz Vensel and Koch Münika.

The trees and plants on the imperial estates included species originating both from Europe and Asia.

Among predominantly formally ladscaped gardens one may see that there were still traces of Ottoman landscaping. In the Bayıldım Bahçe, for example, which is basically a natural grove, one may see traces of a concious effort to create shade, typical of the Turkish garden.

facing page *The pool with a grotto in the Aviary Garden.*
above *A monkey tree in the palace garden.*

THE IMPERIAL TREASURY-HAZİNE-İ HASSA-AND THE FURNISHING MEFRUŞAT CHAMBERS

below *Postcard depicting Dolmabahçe Palace. The building in the foreground is the Mefruşat Dairesi.*
facing page *Postcard depicting the Hazine-i Hassa Dairesi (Office of the Privy Purse) from the sea.*

Both the Treasury chambers and the Furnishing chambers flank the main treasury gate. Access to them is through two small gates flanking the concave wings of the Treasury Gate on either side. The main public entrance to the palace is through one of the flanking gates. The two chambers dominate the entrance façade. Once through their gates, one enters two small courtyards. The courtyard to the right leads to the Treasury Chambers, which overlooks the shore, while the courtyard to the left leads to the Furnishing Chambers-Mefruşat Dairesi. This was the palace's furnishing and supplies office and stores, from where all the hardware and furnishings needed for the palace and its annexes were bought and sold, stored and furnishing planned. It is a two storey building with a total of 900m² working space.

The Treasury Chambers-Hazine-i Hassa Dairesi was the chambers and the entire Ottoman family, including the wives of previous sultans and their offspring, as well as the imperial entourage and staff were carried out. It is also a two storey building with a total working area of 1250m².

Both buildings are quite plain on the exterior,with simple windows piercing the walls and few other noticable features. The interiors are both spacious and decorative, especially in the area of the stairwell.

THE MAIN BUILDING

O n passing through the Treasury Gate into the palace gardens one may enter the main palace building. This is a large monumental structure stretching along the Bosphorus shore, which contains the three main sections of the palace, the Mabeyn-i Hümâyûn and the Harem-i Hümâyûn which occupy two wings flanking the central higher structure-the Ceremonial Hall-Muayade Salon.

Before describing the interior of the palace, we would like to give a general impression of the appearance and style of the exterior.

The massive verticals of the central Ceremonial Hall are countered by predominant horizontals along the two flanking wings of the Harem and the Mabeyn, horizontals broken by columned balconies in the center of each wing. The balconies are surmounted by a classically inspired entablature. Both the

below *The Ceremonial Hall forms the highest section of Dolmabahçe Palace, flanked by the Mabeyn and the Harem. The building next to the Harem is the Veliahd Dairesi (Apartments of the Heir Apparent)* facing page above *View of the Hasbahçe from the Mabeyn Dairesi.*

above *Entrance to the Mabeyn-i Hümâyûn.*
facing page *Entrance to the Mabeyn-i Hümâyûn.*

shore façade, which has been described here as the dominant part of the exterior, and the entrance façade facing the Treasury Gate are elaborately embellished with relief motifs, while the land façade of the Muayede Salon and the Harem are plain by contrast. The ground floor of the palace is pierced by round arched windows, while those of the first storey are surmounted by depressed arches. The upper storey windows are rectangular framed, but alternate with higher arched windows.

The ashlar stone façades are embellished with carved profiles, floriate motifs and garlanded friezes, mainly from the occidental decorative repertoire. There are two main storeys set over a service storey at ground level.

The façades of the Muayede Salon place particular emphasis on the effect of two main storeys, access to the first storey being via a grand flight of curved steps in the Baroque manner, leading up to the grand hall from the quay gate. Round arched windows pierce the façade on this level, alternating with engaged piers, double columns and composite capitals.

The second storey façade, looking onto the gallery, is pierced by round arched paired windows, surmounted in pairs by a broken entablature.

Engaged piers surmounted by double columns and composite capitals alternate between each window. Other decorative features include carved panels and cartouches, medallions and "C" scrolls. In contrast there is little decoration on the land façades of the palace.

The shore façade of the Harem bears great similarity to its twin public wing, while the land façade is articulated simply by rows of different types of arched windows. It is otherwise totally plain.

THE IMPERIAL ADMINISTRATIVE QUARTERS
MABEYN-İ HÜMÂYÛN

A s the visitors cross the palace gardens, they will see a grand entrance before them which opens onto the outside world both physically and functionally.

The Mabeyn was the administrative center of the sultanate, and consists of the Privy Chamber (Resmi-Daire), where the everyday affairs of state were carried out, an audience chamber and ambassadorial suite, where local statesmen and foreign envoys were received by the sultan. This section of the palace was open only to men. It was the first visual encounter to be had by statesmen and envoys of the power of the empire. Hence great pains were taken to ensure that their first impressions would be satisfied, down to every detail of the structure and its decoration.

The main two floors have a similar plan, consisting of three large rooms arranged along the main spinal axis of the building, flanked by smaller rooms leading off from them.

The first of the large rooms is the Medhal Salon, the Main

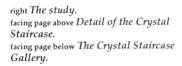

right *The study.*
facing page above *Detail of the Crystal Staircase.*
facing page below *The Crystal Staircase Gallery.*

Reception Hall at entrance level. This room is surrounded by fourteen columns and extends into four annexes. Columns fronting these bay-like annexes form a visual separation from them. The bay facing the main entrance is more extensive than the others, taking on the character ofa portico, which was paved with black and white marble during the residency of the caliph Abdülmecid Efendi. In the spaces between these bays are a number of rooms of different sizes which were used for a variety of purposes. These rooms all open onto the main hall or "sofa" via a corridor or small anteroom. Two of these rooms are notable for their historical connotations-the Grand Vizier's room (No. 6) to the right of the entrance and the Şeyhülislam's (Chief of Religious Administration) room to the left (No. 3).

Ceilings tend to be casetted, or divided into painted squares, with painted tracery motifs within the squares. The walls of the main chambers are embellished by trompe d'oiel motifs-false columns, arches and pilasters. The tangential walls between bays are turned into concave surfaces embellished with decorated fireplaces. The floors are parquet. The second large room on this floor is the stair hall containing the crystal staircase. The

stairwell is enclosed on two sides by walls and a flight of stairs leads down at this point to the lower service floor. The main stair hall is framed around the perimeter by six columns. Somewhat resembling an enclosed balcony it is reached under a triple arch supported by two piers. Entering the palace from the land gate, the first large chamber to be encountered would be the servants' dining room (No. 12). One enters this area via a similar triple arch supported by two piers. Like the crystal stairhall, this room too has the appearance of an enclosed balcony, with six marble glazed columns facing the garden. A flight of stairs leads down from this room direct to the service areas of the palace.

Hence the center of the room is divided by a stairwell, while there are rooms leading off at the corners.

Ceilings in these annexes and flanking rooms tend to be painted with symmetrical panels filled with traced motifs. Only one of the rooms varies from the norm in that it has a barrelvaulted ceiling. This is the room of the Sultan's Chief Eunichs-Musahiban-ı Hazreti Şehriyari Ağaları.

The third main room is the Mounting Room-Binek Salonu. It

facing page and above *The Crystal Staircase.*

above *Detail of the Crystal Staircase Gallery.*
facing page *One of the vases in the Crystal Staircase Gallery.*

has a similar plan to that of the previous hall, although two of the bays-those on the side the Ceremonial Hall-Muayede-are curtailed by the curved interior fireplace wall, but extending towards the light shaft. The bays facing the sea and land façades have access to concealed gates via curved Baroque-style staircases. These bays are provided with a "visual" boundary by a pair of columns at their entrances. Trompe d'oeil pillar and cornices create a seemingly animated wall surface. Some unusual landscape paintings are to be seen among the traced patterns on the ceiling, a feature unique to this room. The floors are parquet throughout.

At this point the symmetricality of the plan is abondoned. The Binek Salon leads to another hall (No. 23), and from there by a corridor to the bedrooms of the Chief Aide (Ser Yâver) and Aides de Camp (Yaveran) (nos. 20&24). It is known that room number 21 was used as a mescid or a prayer room. Another curious room attached to hall no. 23 is a cross-vaulted arched and columned room, which has a balcony above (handing gardens) and kitchens below. This is, at present used as an exhibition area for the permanent exhibition of objects from the palace collection. From here a corridor leads to the map room

which has access to the first floor via a staircase, and a small hall below these stairs gives access to the lower floor and to the passageway leading to the Glazed Pavilion-Camlı Köşk. The corridor is countered by a similar corridor leading to the Ceremonial Hall.

Returning for a moment to the hall of the crystal staircase, on mounting these stairs leading to the first storey, we may see at a glance that this storey bears the same basic plan as the lower storey. Above the entrance hall is the Ambassadorial Hall-Süfera Salonu (room No. 26), which although similar in plan to its

ground floor equivalent, is six-columned. Two columns frame the entrance to the flanking bays on all but the crystal stairwell side. Two rooms, one on either side of the balcony, are among the most important rooms in the palace. Those on the land side (Nos. 27-28) were the Ambassadorial and Translaters' ante-chambers, while the chamber on the shore side (No. 31) was the Ambassadorial Reception Hall- the Crimson Room. Small corner rooms complete the plan. The ceiling is decorated with rows of gilded plaster mouldings which give it a sense of debth. These are geometrical motifs with moulded devices placed

facing page *The Süfera Salon, one of the most opulent rooms in the palace.*
above *The piano bearing the monogram of Sultan Abdülmecid in the Süfera Salon.*

within them. The other small rooms are generally decorated with tracery on the ceiling. The decoration of the main rooms and halls, especially walls and ceilings, has been carried out with much skill and attention to detail, while the use of trompe d'oiel throughout helps to suggest a third dimension. The parquet throughout the hall and its attendant rooms is decorated with foliate and geometrical motifs.

The second large hall on the first storey is the Crystal Staircase (Kristal Merdiven). This stairhall, a spacious area surrounding a grand Baroque staircase bears the distinction of being a nodal point linking to other important halls. The staircess itself, a rectangular area enclosing the crystal staircase with 16 columns is at the center of four bays branching out on four sides. The bays facing the sea and directly inland open into galleries with access through six columns. The others act as connecting bays to the other halls.

Between the bays four corner rooms open onto the hall. One of these, towards the land façade (No.34) is finely decorated with a gilded and fine wood carved, ceiling. Room No.42 is the Somaki Room (Somaki Oda), where the heir elect was given special audience. The walls and ceiling of this room are painted

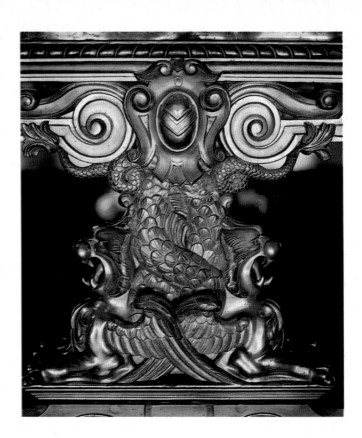

on plaster with false marbling over the walls and ceiling. There are four small chambers around the corner rooms flanking the hall. The two chambers facing on the Ambassadorial Hall side serve as w.c. and coffee service areas while the two facing the Zülvecheyn Hall (Zülvecheyn Salonu) contain concealed staircases. This section has a most noticable painted ceiling. Over the staircase one sees vaulting of Gothic type, while the corridors around the stairwell are also vaulted, with coffered plaster vaulting and low barrel vaulting in the corners.

The Baroque form of the staircase, the focal point of the hall, is emphasised by generous ornamantation in the same style the parquet follows the general pattern of geometrical and foliate motifs.

The third most important room on this level in the public quarters of the palace was the Zülvecheyn-the hall of the privy chamber- which also acted as the ceremonial hall of the Harem. One of the most important rooms in the palace, it has a T-shaped plan. Entering through a double columned bay, one faces the concave wall of the Muayede Salonu. Beyond this point the symmetry of the plan is broken by neccessity, although the rooms flanking this hall are arranged, as before, in opposing pairs branching off the main axis. Two of the rooms

facing page above *The glazed iron roof of the Mabeyn-i Hümâyûn Hamam (baths).*
above and facing page below *Details of the alabaster interior of the Mabeyn-i Hümâyûn Hamam (baths).*

to the land side, the privy dining room (No. 47) and lounge are reached via a corridor. Two roomsfrom the privy chamber on the shore side, a study and prayer room (Nos. 44&45) are adjoined to a third room (No. 43). This modification was carried out during the residency of Abdülmecid the Haliph, to form a library, and now bears the title of the Mecid Efendi Library (Abdülmecid Efendi Kütüphanesi).

Fine gilded stucco mouldings decorate the ceilings of the privy apartment, while the walls are decorated, as in other parts of the palace, with trompe d'oiel architectural effects. The stellar interlace parquet in the Privy Hall are particularly fine, while in the other rooms in the suite foliate and geometrical motifs similar to those seen elsewhere are used on the parquet. A pair of rooms (Nos. 47&49) thought to have been the Sultan's Private Chamber lead via a corridor to a hall (No. 48). Leading off to the right of this hall is another corridor which provides access to tha Imperial Baths and adjoining suite. The three rooms' baths have fine Egyptian alabaster panelling on the walls of the cold and hot rooms. The bath fitments-such as basins, tap surrounds and decorative elements are also of alabaster, which creates a unique effect.

The hall to the other end of the same corridor (No. 48) was known as the Hatıra Salonu. It was used by the Harem, and has access both to the Harem, the Glazed Pavilion and to the lower storey via a staircase which leads to the corridor to the Glazed Pavilion. This extensive corridor, more a spacious passageway, is 81.52 m in length. At the approach to the pavilion, a stairway leads up to an entrance hall, from which two rooms led into the two main chambers of the pavilion, one walled, the other glazed.

The pavilion is T-planned, with a glazed extension supported by columns. The ceiling decorations are quite unusual. A cornice frieze of cartouches around a baldachin-vaulted ceiling contains animal figures. The second chamber, which has glazed roof and walls contains a pool. A typical conservatory in appearance, it was the only window to the outside world in the palace, an imperial observation point.

facing page *The Porphyry Room.*
left *Seaward façade of the Ceremonial Hall.*

THE MUAYEDE SALON - CEREMONIAL HALL

The Ceremonial Hall is at the true center of the palace, between the two main section of palace life, the Harem and the Mabeyn. It is the most impressive room in the palace, large in scale and has a high domed ceiling, reaching through two main storeys. The hall was used for important protocol ceremonies and at Turkish religious state ceremonies. Structurally and functionally plainly quite different from the rest of the palace, it is a centrally-planned area with a domed ceiling supported on four piers. The dome, however, is masked on the exterior by a sloping leaded roof.

The plan indicates a rectangular main area at right-angles to the shore façade flanked by tangential rooms and a series of linking corridors. It has the usual four extending bays which

right and facing page *Details of the Ceremonial Hall façade.*
following pages *The Ceremonial Hall.*

are differentiated from the main area by double columns and round arched niches. Fifty-six additional columns surround the main area, mainly, to decorative effect.

Corner rooms open into the main area, those on the land side being domed while those on the shore side are ceilinged. The latter are linked both to the public and private sections of the palace via corridors.

The gallery overlooking the Ceremonial Hall and extending beyond follows the same general plan as the rest of the palace. The bays of the lower storey are matched by galleries opening out over the main hall between columns.

The hall is lit by windows set in niches on the ground floor and double windows on the gallery level. The windows provide the hall with plenty of natural light. However, the largest

and most elaborate chandelier in the palace is suspended from the dome. 4.5 tons in weight, the chandelier was presented to the palace during the reign of Queen Victoria, and was brought from England. The dome itself and its decoration are striking, trompe d'oiel architectural effects adding stature to the dome on one hand while naturalistic floral compositions and motifs of occidental origin add to the general Baroque effect. Parquet of geometrical design covers the floor throughout.

facing page *Decoration on the dome of the Ceremonial Hall.*
below *The Ceremonial Hall. The 4.5 ton chandelier is of English manufacture.*
following pages *Detail of the Ceremonial Hall.*

THE HAREM-İ HÜMÂYÛN

This was the private family apartments of the sultans, and contained the apartments of the Dowager Sultan, the sultans wives, their entourage and servants.

The Harem had direct access to the Muayede Salon, and consisted of an L-shaped block running parallel to the most complex part of the palace as far as plan and spatial organisation is concerned. This is directly related to the complexity of lifestyle at the Ottoman court. The axial plan of the palace in parallel to the shore façade is generally symmetrical, but in this section the symmetry is broken in relation to the central axis from time to time.

One area on the shore façade linked to the Muayede Salon by a corridor is surmounted by a terrace. This area is split into two by large piers. Now used as Exhibition Room II for objects from the palace collection, it is flanked by a room thought to have been used as a sick room by Abdülmecid (room No. 84) and on the land side by an asymmetrically grouped suite of rooms. A corridor leads from this suite to the first larg ehall of the Harem-the Binek Salon or Mounting Room. A rectangular room with extensive wings facing seaward and landward, the hall has direct access to the exterior via a flight of steps at each end and to the upper floor via a curved staircase known as the Halife Staircase. Corner rooms open ihto the main hall, among them a room known as the Şehzades' Reading Room (room No. 91) another striking room is the so-called Sedefli Oda-Mother-of-Pearl Room (No. 93).

The second large hall in the Harem (No. 96) is a rectangular chamber with the distinction of an extansion stretching up to the shore façade and with an opening onto the shore gardens. There are four columns at the shore entrance. This wing is as wide as the hall itself. A staircase in the corridor linking this hall to its suite of rooms provides access to the upper storey.

The apartments of the Cariyes (Cariyeler Dairesi)-female slaves-and servants were contained in the wing of the Harem which ran at right angles to the main building, and is generally a series of rectangular salons with attendant rooms and suites linked to a central connecting corridor.

facing page *The corridor linking the Mabeyn to the Harem.*
below *One of the stained glass windows in the corridor.*

Hence to general arrangement is a series of communal chambers with service areas and light shafts between, flanked by small rooms and suites with access to the main upper floor via a number of minor staircases. The servants' Quarters are noticably plainer than the upper floors, ceiling decoration being mainly traced geometrical panels.

facing page *The Halife Staircase in the Harem. This staircase leads into the Blue Hall on the upper floor.*
above *The ceiling decoration in the Blue Hall.*

The Blue Hall, one of the main rooms in the Imperial Harem.

above *One of the magnificent doors opening into the Blue Hall.*
facing page above *Corner of the Blue Hall.*
facing page below *The bedroom belonging to the Valide Sultan (sultan's mother) in the Imperial Harem.*

The upper storey of the Harem follows almost the same plan, with some slight variations. The first important room is the Crimson Room (No. 62) which is named after its predominantly red furnishings, the crimson fabric-covered walls in particular. this room is linked to corridor No. 57 which connects the Muayede Salon to the Mabeyn. The first larg espace is known as the Blue Hall (No. 67). A rectangular chamber with

spacious wings over the land and sea façades is the Harem's ceremonial hall. The handsomely coffered ceiling is gilded, the rectangular spaces between decorated with occidental motifs, and embellished with still life and landscape paintings. Trompe d'oiel architectural devices lend apparent depth to the walls. No surface or architectural element, including entablatures over the door is left undecorated. One of the corner rooms opening onto the Blue room is the bedchamber of Sultan Abdülaziz (No. 73) on the land side, while on the shore façade are a bedroom (No. 63) and a room used by Atatürk as his study (No. 69). Room No. 71 in the same suit is the room where Atatürk died.

facing page *Corner of the Pink Room.*
above *Atatürk's study.*
below *Atatürk's bedroom.*

The Harem's second most important and largest salon is the rectangular Pink Room, used as Atatürk's private suite.

The casetted ceiling and false painted columns are among the interesting features of this room. A corridor (No. 109) leads from this room to link up with another corridor at right angles to the shore façade and leads to the Harem Baths. The two corridors are separated by a door. The baths contains a hot room, a cold room, a rest room and a toilet. The tiles in the hot and cold rooms are particularly notable.

above and right *Details of the Harem Hamam (baths).*
facing page above *A bedroom in the Harem.*
facing page left *Detail of the bedspread in the same bedroom.*
facing page right *View of the garden from the Harem.*

The upper storey of the Cariyes' Quarters, the wing of the Harem at right angles to the main palace, is identical in plan to the ground floor. One room is noticably different from the others in the elaborateness of its decoration, the corner room at the end of the building.

The walls and ceilings in the servants' quarters are generally simple, almost undecorated, parquet is used sparingly and without embellishment, the floors being mainly covered by straw matting. These features are, in themselves, interesting.

THE VELİAHD DAİRE
HEIRS ELECT APARTMENTS

This is a separate section of the palace, contained within the Harem extension wing but cut off from the Harem proper, with an entrance of its own, and its own gardens surrounded by walls isolating it from the palace grounds. These were the apartments of the crown prince selected for succession.

The plan and façade of this wing area repeat, on a smaller scale, of those of the main building. The apartments include a

Selamlık or a male quarters, a Ceremonial Hall or *Muayede* and a *Harem*. Like the main building it has two main storeys and a service floor at ground level. The main entrance is via a stepped portal on the side of the building facing the Servants' quarters to the north. The building has an axial plan, the Med-hal-Entrance Hall-is linked via a number of corridors to the Ceremonial Hall-Muayede Salonu. The latter is a grand and spacious area whose presence in the building is felt on the sea and land façades by monumental columns and friezes. This in turn connects to the Harem in the main building via various corridors. The ground floor plan is repeated on the upper storey. The two storeys are linked by a grand staircase similar to the Halife stairs in the main building. Apart from service staircases, the only major links between floors are this, which rises from the northern corridor of the Muayede Salon, and a staircase in the Medhal Salon.

The façade facing the main Harem building is blind, but decorated with false windows. The Veliahd Daire became the Museum of Art and Sculpture in modern times (by the 1937 decree of Atatürk).

facing page *View of Dolmabahçe from Beşiktaş. The building in the foreground adjoining the palace is the Veliahd Daire (Apartments of the Heir Apparent).*
below *The vaulted staircase of the Veliahd Daire.*

THE HAREKET KÖŞKS

The pavilions-köşks-set in their own grounds and separated from the Veliahd Apartments garden by a low wall were built towards the end of the 19th century. They are thought to have been constructed after the strong earthquakes which shook the city at that time, and to be named after the

word "Hareket"-quake. Both are wooden. The köşk adjacent to the Veliahd Daire's high wall, known as the "first" was meant to be the male quarters while the second köşk, which is linked to the Chief Eunuch's apartments, was arranged as the Harem quarters. These buildings are highly reminiscent of French or Swiss alpine chalets with hipped roofs and characteristic façades.

THE APARTMENTS OF THE CHIEF EUNUCH
KIZLARAĞASI DAİRESİ

This is reached via a bridge directly behind the second Hareket Köşk. It is a two storeyed building, and contains the private apartments of the most high ranking officer in the Harem, who was responsible for its administration. It is isolated from the main building by a high wall. One interesting feature of the building is the marble-revetted baths on the first floor. This building now houses a number of workshops whose presence in the palace is a tradition.

facing page *The back garden of the Veliahd Daire and the Hareket Köşks built during the reign of Abdülhamid II.*
left *Interior of the Hareket Köşks.*

THE SERVANTS' APARTMENTS
MUSÂHİBÂN DAİRESİ

This is a separate building, part of the third and last group of buildings in the complex, following the main building and the Veliahd Apartments in linear succession from Kabataş towards Beşiktaş. The building is rectangular, the house has a sea façade and its own garden.

This simple and charming building was reserved for favoured individuals in the sultan's service. It is now the Beşiktaş district governor's office-Kaymakam-and the Transport Regional Offices.

BENDEGÂN AND AGAVAT APARTMENTS
SLAVES AND EUNUCHS

This two storeyed building wedged between the Musahiban-Servants' Apartments and the Guards Apartments Baltacılar has a tiny inner court for the use of the slaves and eunuchs. Although retaining the characteristic outline of its original exterior, the building is thoroughly restored, and is at present used as the archives of the Naval Museum.

BALTACILAR APARTMENTS
PRIVY GUARD

These quarters are situated facing Dolmabahçe Caddesi towards Akaretler and behind the Bendegân and Agavat Daire. It has two main storeys over a basal service level. Originally allocated to the privy guard, a section of the imperial entourage with administrative as well as protective duties, it is now in use as the Conservatory of Mimar Sinan University.

Matbâh-ı Âmire-Imperial Kitchen

The penultimate group of buildings within the palace enclosure is that closest to the Barbaros Jetty at Beşiktaş. The kitchens are housed in the outermost of those buildings. We know that French and Italian chefs worked in the palace kitchens, which are now no longer recognisable as kitchens. The photographic documentations shows that little of the present building is original.

Auxiliary Buildings

A group of buildings on the slopes of what was the Bayıldım Bahçesi, north of the palace upshore was used to supply the court with many of its needs. It was a little complex of palace industries containing everything the palace might need, from pharmacy to confectioners, flour mill to grain store, bakery to blacksmith. Tha complex faced out onto Dolmabahçe Caddesi, its two storey façade presenting a dignified foil to the Akaretler Apartments of the Sultan Abdülaziz period.

Clock Tower

The clock tower stands outside the Treasury Gate (Hazine Kapı). It was built in 1890-1891, after the palace had been completed, during the reign of Abdülhamid II.

The tower is set on a rectangular base, with fountains on the

basal walls. The broad first storey is pierced by a door surmounted with barometres. Each face of the top storey contains
a clock. Surrounding the uppermost storey is a balustrade and

surmounting it a finial. The decoration of the tower is eclectic in style, the windows are flanked by double columns and elaborate devices are used throughout.

previous pages and above *Views of Dolmabahçe Clock Tower.*

BIBLIOGRAPHY

AHMET REFİK (ALTINAY), *Hicri Onikinci Asırda İstanbul Hayatı*, İstanbul, 1930.

ALLOM T. - WALSH B., *Constantinople and the Scenery of the Seven Churches of Asia Minor*, London, 1835-1840.

AMICIS, E. de *Constantinople*, Paris, 1878.

AREL, A., *18. Yüzyıl İstanbul Mimarisinde Batılılaşma Süreci*, İstanbul, 1975.

ATASOY, N., "Dolmabahçe Sarayı'nın Türk Karakteri", *Milli Saraylar Sempozyumu-Bildiriler*, İstanbul, 1985, p. 85-89.

Başbakanlık Arşivi, *Cevdet Saray*, 7 R., 1265, ref. no. 4103.

Başbakanlık Arşivi, *Cevdet Saray*, ref. no. 4431, 282, 1223 takrir.

Başbakanlık Arşivi, *Cevdet Saray*, 26 R., 1265, ref. no. 5785.

Başbakanlık Arşivi, *İrade Hariciye*, no. 7184, 7188, 8795/3.

BERK, N., "Le Palais de Dolmabahçe", *Türkiye Turing ve Otomobil Kurumu Belleteni*, no. 249 (1962), p. 24-25.

CEVDET PAŞA, *Tezakir*, (Yayın. Prof. Cavit Baysun) no. 1-40, Ankara, 1986.

CEZAR, M., *Sanatta Batıya Açılış ve Osman Hamdi*, İstanbul, 1971.

CEZAR, M., "Sanatta Batıya Açılışta Saray Yapıları ve Kültürün Yeri", *Milli Saraylar Sempozyumu-Bildiriler*, İstanbul, 1985, p. 45-69.

D'OHSSON, M., *Tableau Général de L'Empire Ottoman*, vol. III, Paris, 1787-1820.

ELDEM, S.H., *Türk Evi Plan Tipleri*, İ.T.Ü. Mimarlık Fakültesi, 1968.

ELDEM, S.H., *Köşkler ve Kasırlar*, vol. II, İstanbul, 1974.

ELDEM, S.H., *İstanbul Anıları*, vol. II, İstanbul, 1979.

ERDENEN, O., "Çağlar Boyunca Boğaziçi", *Hayat Tarih Mecmuası*, vol. II, no. 8 (1968), p. 48-49.

ERGİN, O., *Mecelle-i Umur-u Belediye*, vol. III, 1330-1335, p. 367-373.

ETİNGÜ, T., "Dolmabahçe Sarayı", *Hayat Tarih Mecmuası*, vol. I, no. 1, (1966), p. 42-48.

EVLİYA ÇELEBİ, *Seyahatnâme*, İstanbul, 1314, I (New Edition Evliya Çelebi Seyahatnâmesi II, İstanbul, trans. Zuhuri Danışman).

EVYAPAN, A. G., *Eski Türk Bahçeleri ve Özellikle Eski İstanbul Bahçeleri*, Ankara, 1972.

EYİCE, S., *İstanbul*, Petit Guide à Travers les Monuments Byzantins et Turcs, İstanbul, 1955.

EYİCE, S., *Bizans Devrinde Boğaziçi*, İstanbul, 1976.

FONTMAGNE, D., *Kırım Harbi Sonrasında İstanbul*, İstanbul, 1977.

GAUTIER, T., *İstanbul* (trans. N. Berk)-(undated), p. 263-269.

GOODWIN, G., *A. History of Ottoman Architecture*, London-Baltimore, 1971.

GÜLERSOY, Ç., *Dolmabahçe Sarayı*, İstanbul, 1967.

GÜLERSOY, Ç., *Dolmabahçe Sarayı*, İstanbul Kitaplığı, 1984.

GÜLERSOY, Ç., "Dolmabahçe Sarayı", Türkiyemiz, no. 11, (1973).

HAFIZ HIZIR İLYAS AĞA, Tarih-i Enderun/Letaif-i Enderun, (trans. Cahit Kayra), İstanbul, 1987.

HAMMER, J. Von, *Osmanlı Devleti Tarihi*, (Trans. from original by Mehmet Ata Bey. Publ. M. Çevik and E. Kılıç), vol. I-XII, İstanbul, 1983-1986.

HAUTECCEUR, L., *Historie de l'Architecture Classique en France*, vol. III, Paris, 1957, p. 264.

HASOL, D., *Ansiklopedik Mimarlık Sözlüğü*, İstanbul, 1979.

HUTTON, W.H., *Constantinople, The History of The Old Capital of the Empire*, London, 1900.

İNCİCİYAN, P., *18. Yüzyılda İstanbul*, (trans. H. Andreasyan) İstanbul, 1976.

JANIN, R., *Constantinople Byzantine, Development Urbain et Répertoire Topographique*, Paris, 1890.

KARAL, E.Z., *Osmanlı Tarihi*, vol. VI-VII, Ankara, 1977.

KOÇU, R.E., "Evliya Çelebi Seyahatnamesinde Boğaziçi" paragraph, *İstanbul Ansiklopedisi*, vol.V, İstanbul, 1961, p. 2856.

KONYALI, İ.H., *İstanbul Abidelerinden: İstanbul Sarayları*, İstanbul, 1943.

KÖMÜRCÜYAN, E.Ç., *17. Asırda İstanbul*, (trans. H. Andreasyan) İstanbul, 1988.

KUBAN, D., *Türk Barok Mimarisi Hakkında Bir Deneme*, İstanbul, 1954.

MAMBOURY, E., *İstanbul Turistique*, İstanbul, 1952.

(Mrs.) MAX MÜLLER, M., *İstanbul'dan Mektuplar*, İstanbul, 1978.

MELLING, M., *Voyage Pittoresque de Constantinople et des rives du Bosphore*, İstanbul, 1969.

MEREY, Ş.L., "Dolmabahçe Sarayı Muayede Salonu'nun Isıtma Donatımı", *İ.D.M.M. Akademisi Dergisi 4*, off print, 1978.

Milli Saraylar Arşivi, *İrade-i Seniye Kayıt Defteri*, 2670, ref. no. 614.

Milli Saraylar Arşivi, *Evrak I*, 1383.

Milli Saraylar Dergisi, no. 1, 1987/1, İstanbul.

MİNASYAN, A., *Osmanlı Sarayının Mimarlığını Yapan Balyan Sülalesi*, İstanbul, 1973 (İ.Ü. Edebiyat Fakültesi Sanat Tarihi Bölümü, Unpublished undergraduate thesis).

MOLTKE, H. Von, *Türkiye Mektupları*, (trans. H. Örs), İstanbul, 1969.

NEAVE, D. L., *Eski İstanbul'da Hayat*, (trans. O. Öndeş), İstanbul, 1978.

NEAVE, D. L., *Twenty Six Years on Bosphorous*, London, 1933.

OLCAY-EGE, Y., *Dolmabahçe Sarayı Dış ve İç Süslemeleri*, Ankara, 1978 (H.Ü. Sosyal ve İdari Bilimler Fak., Unpublished M.A. thesis).

OSMANOĞLU, A., *Babam Abdülhamit*, İstanbul, 1960.

ÖZTUNA. Y., *Büyük Türkiye Tarihi*, vol. VII, İstanbul, 1978.

PAKALIN, E.Z., *Osmanlı Tarihi Deyimleri ve Terimleri Sözlüğü*, (III Cilt), M.E.B. Publ.

PAMUKCİYAN, K., "Karabet Balyan", *İstanbul Ansiklopedisi*, vol. IV, İstanbul, 1960.

PAMUKCİYAN, K., "Nikogos Balyan", *İstanbul Ansiklopedisi*, vol. IV, İstanbul, 1960.

PARDOE, J., *The Beauties of the Bosphorus*, London, 1838.

POUQUEVILLE, F.C.H.L., *Voyage en Morée, à Constantinople, en Albanie*, vol. II, Paris, MDCCCV, p. 27-28, 200-207.

REYHANLI, T., *İngiliz Gezginlerine Göre XVI. Yüzyılda İstan-*

bul'da Hayat, Ankara, 1983.

SAZ, L., *Haremin İçyüzü*, İstanbul, 1974.

SERTOĞLU, M., *Resimli Osmanlı Tarihi Ansiklopedisi*, İstanbul, 1958.

SERTOĞLU, M., "Dolmabahçe'den Beşiktaş'a", *Hayat Tarih Mecmuası*, vol. II, no. 9, 1977, p. 66-77.

SEVENGİL, R. A., *Saray Tiyatrosu*, İstanbul, 1962.

SİLAHDAR FINDIKLILI MEHMET AĞA, *Silahdar Tarihi*, vol. I, p. 732.

SÖZEN, M., *Türk Mimarisinin Gelişimi ve Mimar Sinan*, İstanbul, 1975.

ŞEHSUVAROĞLU, H., "Dolmabahçe Sarayı", *Arkitekt*, no. 46/173-174, 1946, p. 127-130.

ŞEHSUVAROĞLU, H., *Sultan Aziz'in Hayatı, Hal'i, Ölümü*, İstanbul, 1949.

ŞEHSUVAROĞLU, H., "Le Palais de Dolmabahçe", *Türkiye Turing ve Otomobil Kurumu Belleteni*, no. 102 (1950), p. 24-26.

ŞEHSUVAROĞLU, H., "La Salle d'Audience des Ambassadeurs au Palais Dolmabahtché", *Türkiye Turing ve Otomobil Kurumu Belleteni*, no. 126 (1952), p. 28-29.

ŞEHSUVAROĞLU, H., *Tarihi Odalar*, İstanbul, 1954.

ŞEHSUVAROĞLU, H., *Asırlar Boyunca İstanbul, Sarayları, Abideleri, Çeşmeleri*, Cumhuriyet Gazetesi Historical Magazine, 1954.

ŞEHSUVAROĞLU, H., "Souvenirs d'un Hall du Palais de Dolmabahçe" *Türkiye Turing ve Otomobil Kurumu Belleteni* no. 219-222 (1960) p. 21-22.

ŞEHSUVAROĞLU, H., "Milli Saraylar", *Türkiye Turing ve Otomobil Kurumu Belleteni* no. 264 (1964).

Takvim-i Vekayi, 26 N. 1260, no. 273.

Takvim-i Vekayi, 5 N. 1258, no. 246.

Takvim-i Vekayi, 4 Ca. 1260, no. 270.

TBMM Milli Saraylar Sempozyumu-Bildiriler, İstanbul, 1985.

TOKAY, M., "Dolmabahçe Sarayı", *Türkiye Turing ve Otomobil Kurumu Belleteni* no. 195 (1958) p. 26-27.

TURANİ, A., *Dünya Sanat Tarihi*, Ankara, 1971.

UŞAKLIGİL, H.Z., *Saray ve Ötesi*, vol. III, Ankara, 1941

UZUNÇARŞILI, İ.H., *Osmanlı Devletinin Saray Teşkilatı*, Ankara, 1945.

ÜNSAL, B. "İstanbul'un İmarı ve Eski Eser Kaybı", *Türk Sanatı Tarihi Araştırma ve İncelemeleri II*, İstanbul, 1969, p. 6-61.

ÜNVER, S., "Bir Beşiktaş Sarayı Vardı", *Hayat Tarihi Mecmuası*, vol. II, no. 10, (1967), p. 12.

WOODS, H., *Türkiye Anıları*, (Çev. Amiral F. Çoker), İstanbul, 1976.

YÜCEL, İ.,-ÖNER, S., *Dolmabahçe Sarayı*, TBMM Vakfı Publ. (undated).